P9-DEC-029

THANK YOU

ty

Written & Compiled by **Amelia Riedler**
Designed by **Sarah Forster**

When we're presented with an act of generosity

—whether it's a small encouragement, a much-needed word of support, or a big favor—we've been given a gift that helps keep us going, that lifts us up, and that makes our life better.

When we pause and take a closer look at these gifts, we clearly see the kind people who make these good things happen. We recognize the thoughtful people in our lives who make a difference.

And we realize just how much we need to say thank you.

We must find time

to stop and thank the people who make a difference in our lives.

• John F. Kennedy •

I can no other
answer make, but
THANKS,
and thanks...

• William Shakespeare •

What a difference ONE PERSON can make!

• Unknown •

SOME PEOPLE STRENGTHEN
our society just by being the kind of people they are.

• John W. Gardner •

Realize
HOW GOOD
you really are.

• Og Mandino •

GOOD PEOPLE
increase the value of
EVERY OTHER PERSON
they influence in any way.

• Kelly Ann Rothaus •

The people who
MAKE A DIFFERENCE
are not the ones with the credentials,
BUT THE ONES
with the concern.

• Max Lucado •

Some pursue happiness,
others create it.

• Unknown •

UNSELFISH ACTS
are the real miracles out of which
all the reported
MIRACLES
GROW.

• Ralph Waldo Emerson •

He who wishes to
SECURE THE
GOOD OF OTHERS
has already secured his own.

• Confucius •

The smallest
ACT OF
KINDNESS
is worth more than
THE GRANDEST
INTENTION.

• Oscar Wilde •

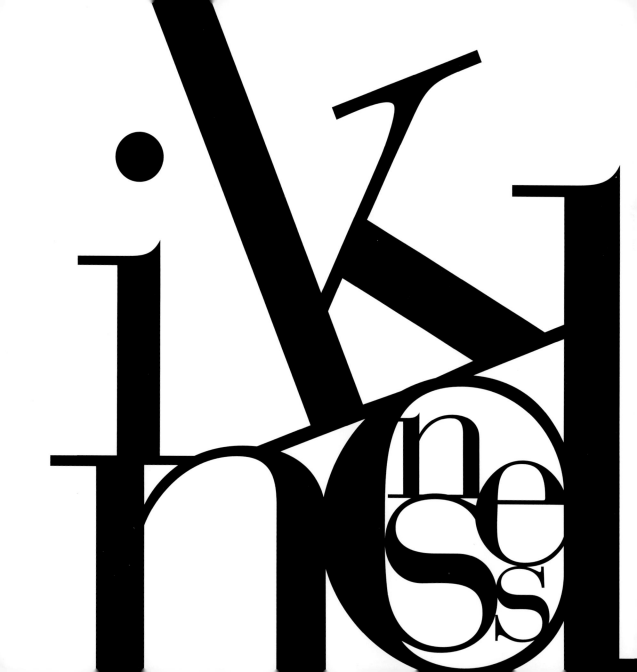

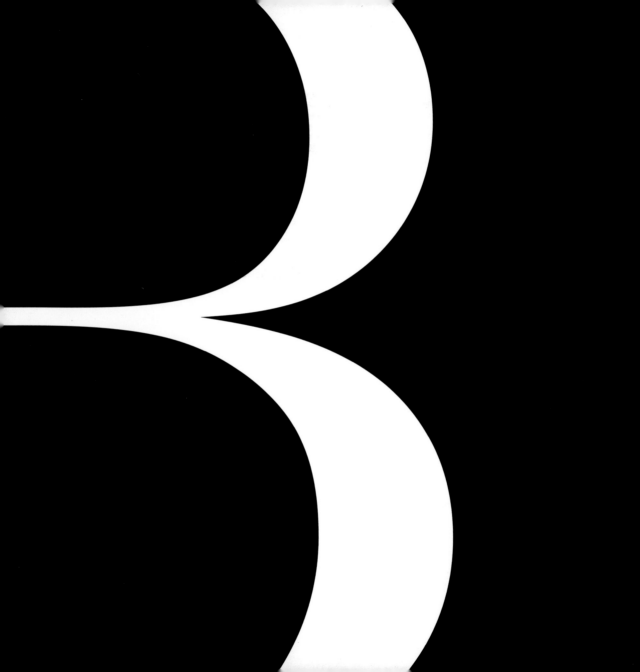

Really big PEOPLE

are, above everything else, courteous, considerate **AND GENEROUS** —not just to some people in some circumstances— but to everyone all the time.

• Thomas J. Watson Sr. •

MAY HAPPINESS
touch your life today
as warmly as you have
touched the lives of others.

• Rebecca Forsythe •

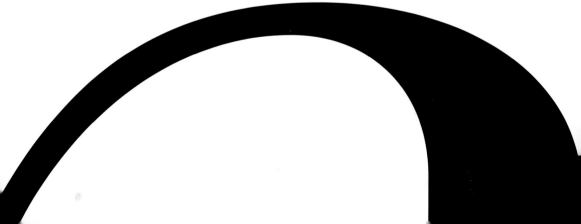

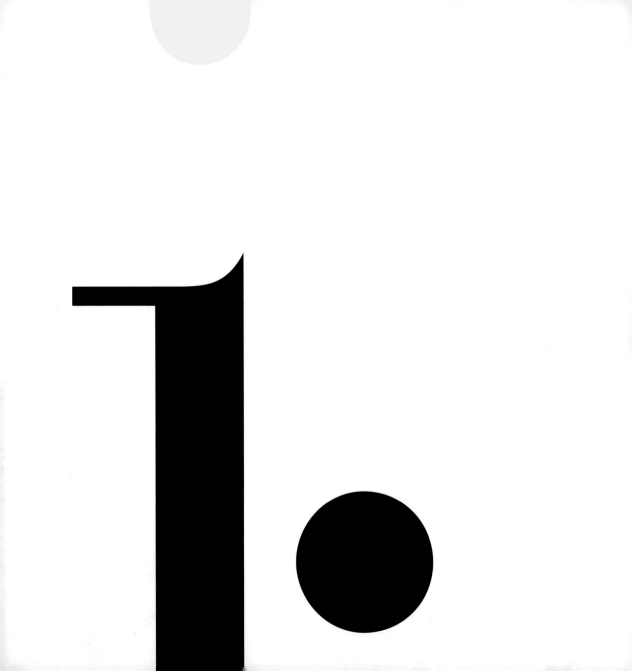

THE EFFECT OF ONE GOOD-HEARTED PERSON
is incalculable.

• Oscar Arias •

YOU GIVE MUCH
and know not that you give at all.

• Kahlil Gibran •

THERE ARE PEOPLE WHOM ONE
loves and appreciates
IMMEDIATELY AND FOREVER.

• Nancy Spain •

For all that has been,
THANKS.
For all that will be,
YES.

• Dag Hammarskjöld •

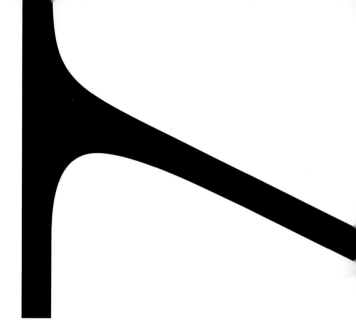

By being yourself,
you put something wonderful in the
world that was not there before.

• Edwin Elliot •

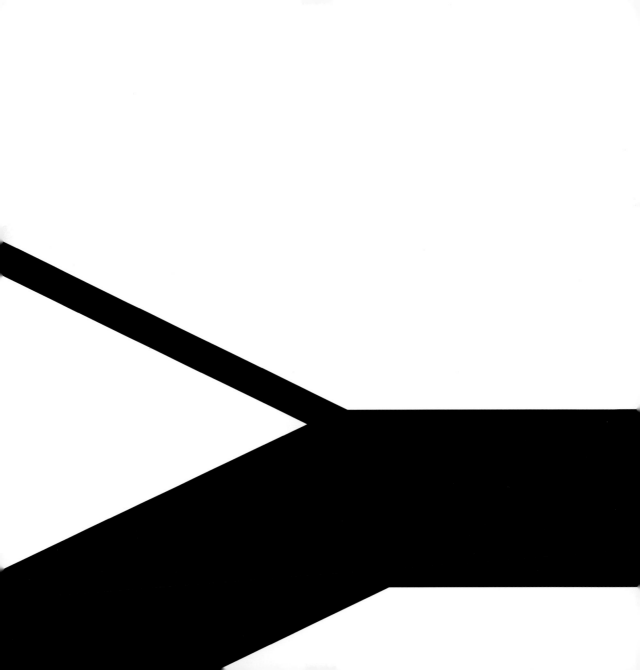

I thank you for your
KINDNESS,
I will not soon forget.

• Joanna Fuchs •

It's not what
WE HAVE IN OUR LIFE,
but who
WE HAVE IN OUR LIFE
that counts.

• J.M. Laurence •

Let us be grateful
to people who make us
HAPPY...

• Marcel Proust •

Those who bring
SUNSHINE
to the lives of others
cannot keep it from
themselves.

• J.M. Barrie •

THANK YOU
for being.

• Native American Greeting •

A GOOD PERSON is a gift to the whole WORLD.

• Heidi Wills •

May the joy
that you give to others
be the joy that
comes back to you.

• Unknown •

COMPENDIUM.
live inspired

WITH SPECIAL THANKS TO
THE ENTIRE COMPENDIUM FAMILY.

CREDITS:

Written & Compiled by: **Amelia Riedler**

Designed by: **Sarah Forster**

Edited by: **M.H. Clark**

Creative Direction by: **Julie Flahiff**

ISBN: 978-1-938298-30-1

© 2013 by Compendium, Inc. All rights reserved. No part of this publication may be reproduced or transmitted in any form or by any means, electronic or mechanical, including photocopy, recording, or any storage and retrieval system now known or to be invented without written permission from the publisher. Contact: Compendium, Inc., 2100 North Pacific Street, Seattle, WA 98103. *Thank You*; Compendium; live inspired; and the format, design, layout, and coloring used in this book are trademarks and/or trade dress of Compendium, Inc. This book may be ordered directly from the publisher, but please try your local bookstore first. Call us at 800.91.IDEAS, or come see our full line of inspiring products at live-inspired.com.

4th printing. Printed in China with soy inks.